GET TO KNOW
YOUR PET

Rats and Mice

**JINNY
JOHNSON**

W
FRANKLIN WATTS
LONDON•SYDNEY

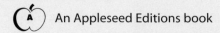 An Appleseed Editions book

First published in 2008 by Franklin Watts
338 Euston Road, London NW1 3BH

Franklin Watts Australia
Hachette Children's Books
Level 17/207 Kent St, Sydney, NSW 2000

© 2008 Appleseed Editions

Created by Appleseed Editions Ltd,
Well House, Friars Hill, Guestling,
East Sussex TN35 4ET

Designed by Guy Callaby
Edited by Mary-Jane Wilkins
Illustrations by Bill Donohoe
Picture research by Su Alexander

Thanks to Richard, James, Ella, Simon and Joe
for their help and advice

ISBN 978 07496 8063 3

Dewey Classification: 636.935

A CIP catalogue for this book is available from the British Library.

Picture acknowledgements
page 5 Juniors Bildarchiv/OSF; 7 Bsip/OSF; 8 LWA-Paul
Chmielowiec/Corbis; 10 Juniors Bildarchive/OSF; 13 Survival
Anglia/OSF; 19 Juniors Bildarchiv/OSF; 20 Steve Gorton/Getty
Images; 24 Juniors Bildarchiv/OSF
Front cover Arco Images/Alamy

Printed in China

Franklin Watts is a division of Hachette Children's Books

Contents

Rats and mice

Rats and mice make excellent pets for all the family. Some people think they are dirty and dangerous, but they are not. Pet rats and mice are clean, safe animals and do not carry disease.

Rats and mice belong to a group of animals called rodents. Pet mice are related to the wild house mouse and pet rats to the brown rat. Rats and mice live in groups in the wild, so if you keep them as pets in groups of two or three they won't get bored or lonely. But never keep rats and mice together in the same cage.

MOUSE

Body features

- Long tail to help with balance and climbing.
- Strong front teeth which grow throughout life.
- Long whiskers which help the animal find out about its surroundings.
- Smooth furry coat.

RAT

A rat has a larger, heavier body than a mouse.

PET SUBJECT

Q **Which make better pets – rats or mice?**

A Both make good pets in different ways. Rats are very intelligent and friendlier than mice. They are easier to tame and can become attached to their owners. Rats don't move quite as fast as mice so they can be easier to hold and handle. But mice are lots of fun too and good to watch as they play in their cage. Mice don't need as much time and exercise outside the cage as rats, so they can be easier and less time consuming to look after.

RODENT FACT
Mice live for about two years and rats for two to three years.

Rats and mice make friendly playful pets, always ready for some fun.

A day in the life

Wild rats and mice are most active at night. Pet rats and mice sleep for more than half the day, often in short bursts, and are generally most lively in the evening.

Rats and mice like to play at night, too, so it's important for them to have each other's company when you are asleep.

While they are awake, rats and mice spend several hours grooming themselves and each other. They need plenty of exercise. Rats especially need time out of their cage every day to run around and explore. Make sure they have toys such as cardboard tubes, wheels and hidey-holes inside their cage too.

Finding food

Wild mice and rats spend most of their waking hours finding food. You will give your pets all their food, but they can still enjoy hunting for titbits. Hide some treats in a cardboard box or a loo roll tube that the animals have to chew their way into.

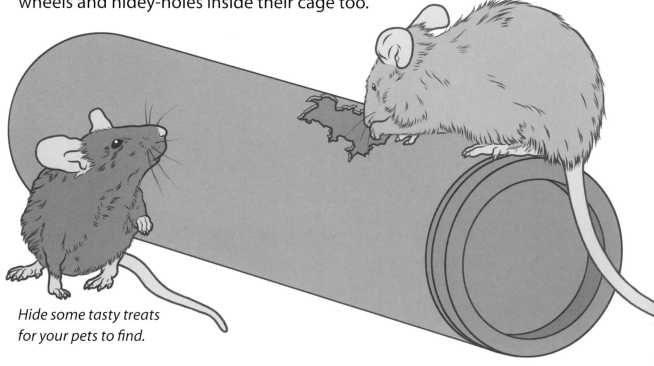

Hide some tasty treats for your pets to find.

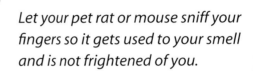

RAT FACT
A group of rats is called a mischief.

Let your pet rat or mouse sniff your fingers so it gets used to your smell and is not frightened of you.

PET SUBJECT

Q **Will a pet rat or mouse become really tame?**

A Yes, it will if you treat it well and give it lots of time and attention. A rat is much more likely to become tame enough to sit on your lap or ride on your shoulder, but mice can be very friendly too. The important thing is for the animal to learn that it can trust you to be kind and gentle.

Rat and mouse senses

Wild rats and mice are prey animals. This means they are always on the alert for cats, dogs and other predators. Your pet mouse or rat may be perfectly safe in your home, but it will still feel the need to watch for danger.

These animals are most active at night and depend more on their sharp ears and sensitive nose than on their eyes. Rats and mice also use their whiskers to explore their surroundings. Their whiskers constantly brush against things as the animals move around.

PET SUBJECT

Q Why is my mouse always twitching its whiskers?

A Touching things with their whiskers helps mice and rats find out about their surroundings. They can probably tell more about things that are close to them with their whiskers than with their eyes. Their whiskers help them to find their way in the dark and to check whether they can fit through an opening. They also help them judge whether food is good to eat or not. Rats can even move the whiskers on one side of the head separately from those on the other side.

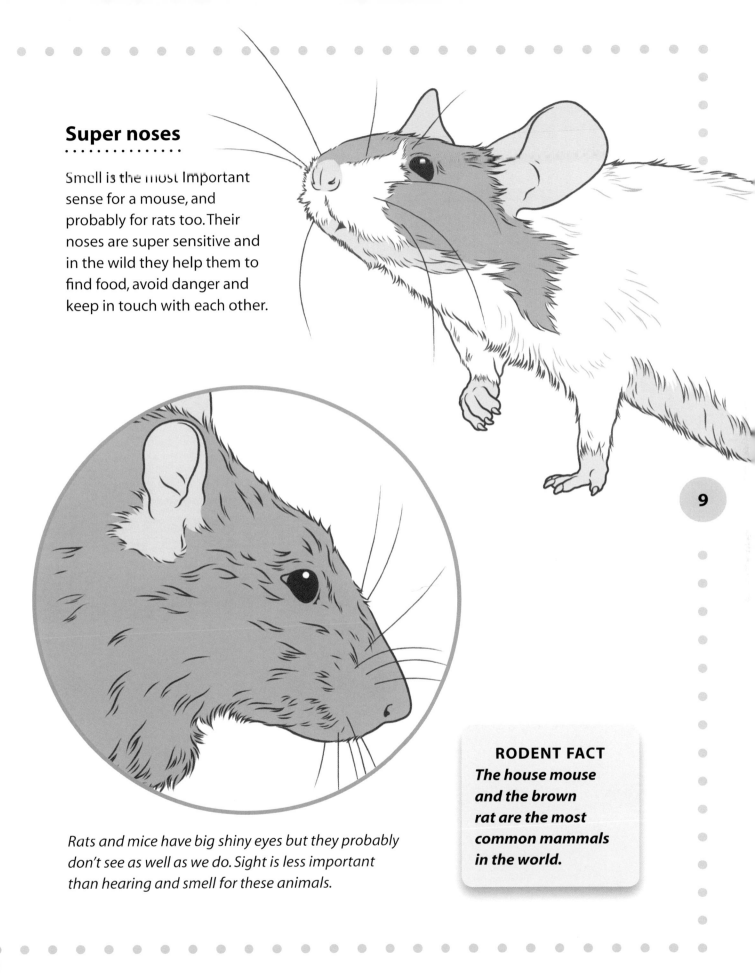

Super noses

Smell is the most Important sense for a mouse, and probably for rats too. Their noses are super sensitive and in the wild they help them to find food, avoid danger and keep in touch with each other.

9

Rats and mice have big shiny eyes but they probably don't see as well as we do. Sight is less important than hearing and smell for these animals.

RODENT FACT
The house mouse and the brown rat are the most common mammals in the world.

Kinds of rats and mice

Pet rats can be lots of different colours, such as black, blue-grey and many shades of brown and white. Some are all one colour; others are a mixture of white and other colours.

Most rats have black eyes, but white rats have pink eyes. Rats have smooth short fur, but a type called the Rex has a curly coat.

Mice can be similar colours and there are many beautiful varieties, including silvery grey mice with a darker tail and ears, and dark chocolate-coloured mice. Most mice have short fur like rats, but there are some long-haired mice.

RAT FACT
Brown rats originally came from northern China and Mongolia, but they have spread all over the world and live everywhere that humans do.

If you want to see lots of different pet rats you might like to go to a rat show.
See website on page 31

There are more than 40 different kinds of pet mouse in a range of attractive colours.

Boy or girl?

Keep pairs of the same sex – otherwise your pets will have babies every few weeks. Two female mice will be happy together and make easier pets than two males. Male mice may fight and are smellier than females. Both male and female rats make good pets and should get on well, particularly if they are brothers or sisters. Females tend to be livelier than males and easier to train.

PET SUBJECT

Q **Why do mice squeak?**

A Generally mice are quiet animals and don't make many sounds. They may squeak if they are afraid or angry. Rats, too, rarely squeak unless they are in pain or upset. They make other sounds to communicate with each other, but these are too high-pitched for humans to hear.

Choosing your rat or mouse

You can buy rats and mice from a pet shop or a breeder. If you want to buy from a breeder, ask your vet or local animal welfare organization to recommend one.

Wherever you buy rats and mice, make sure the animals are healthy and well cared for. Look at their cages and check that they are clean. Animals that have been well looked after and handled from a young age will be easy to tame and not scared of people. Mice should be at least five weeks old before leaving their mother, and rats should be six weeks old.

What to look for

- A smooth shiny coat with no bald patches or lumps.
- Clear bright eyes.
- Quiet breathing with no wheezing or sneezing.
- A playful animal which is not afraid of people.
- Teeth and nails which are not too long.
- Be warned: a very plump rat or mouse might be pregnant!

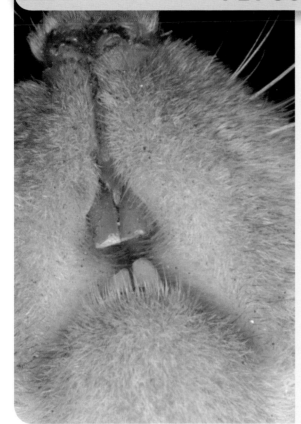

PET SUBJECT

Q **Why do rats and mice have such big front teeth?**

A Wild rats and mice need big, strong front teeth because they spend a lot of time chewing. They eat tough food such as seeds and they gnaw through hard materials such as wood to get at food. Their teeth keep growing so they don't get worn down. A rodent couldn't eat if its teeth were ground down.

13

RAT FACT
A male rat is called a buck and a female is a doe. Baby rats are called kittens or pups.

Always make sure your pets have something hard to chew.

A home for your pets

Mice and rats are lively, active animals and they need plenty of space to move around. Make sure your pets' cage is as big as possible and keep it indoors, away from direct sunlight and draughts.

Rats need a larger cage than mice, with plenty of room to run around and climb. A wire cage with a plastic base is best for rats. It should measure at least 50 x 80 cm and 50 cm high. Rats should always be able to stand up if they want to, and they like to climb so a tall cage is a good idea. Never buy a cage with a wire base as this can injure the rats' feet.

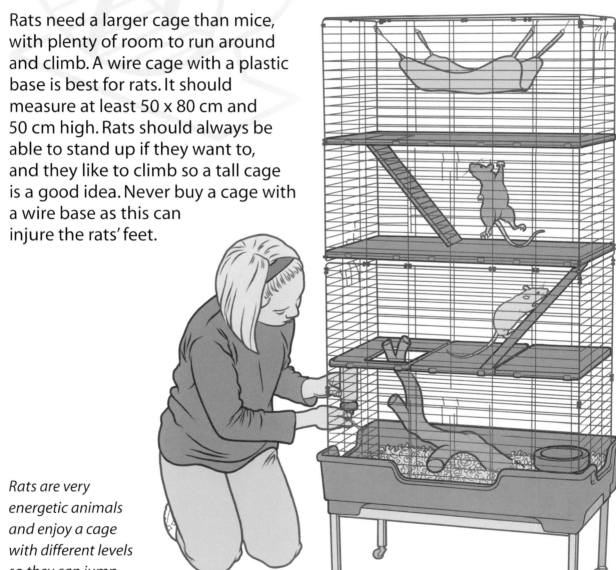

Rats are very energetic animals and enjoy a cage with different levels so they can jump and climb.

There are many types of cage for mice. The best type is a wire cage with a plastic base, or a glass or plastic tank with a wire lid to give the mice plenty of air. Two mice need a cage that measures at least 60 x 50 cm and is 30 cm tall.

If you use a glass or plastic cage make sure your pets have enough air.

Extras

Your pets will also need food bowls. Good heavy bowls made of earthenware are best, as they do not tip over easily. And you will need a drip-feed water bottle that fits on the side of the cage so your pets always have clean water to drink. Rats and mice like a nest box in their cage where they can hide away when they want to and sleep in peace.

PET SUBJECT

Q **Why do some rats have red tears in their eyes?**

A Rats sometimes have red drops around the eyes. This is not blood but comes from special glands and can be a sign that your pet is not well, or is stressed. Perhaps it does not have enough space – is it living in too small a cage or with too many other rats? It's best to check with a vet to find out what might be wrong.

Preparing your pets' home

Your rats and mice will wee and poo in their home, so you need to put some absorbent material on the floor. Line the cage with newspaper and add some bedding.

Bedding can be shredded cardboard, recycled shredded paper, wood litter pellets or dust-extracted wood shavings. Always buy bedding from a pet shop and check that it is suitable for rodents. Never use sawdust or ordinary wood shavings, which can be harmful to rodents and contains dust that affects their breathing. Fill the nest box with shredded tissue or kitchen paper.

Cleaning the cage

Check your pets' cage every day and take out any leftover food and dirty bedding. Give the cage a thorough clean every week. Remove the bedding and lining, wash the cage and put in new bedding. You might like to leave a little of the old bedding so it smells familiar. If you keep your pets' home clean they won't smell bad.

Keep your pets' cage clean so they stay healthy and happy.

Put some toys in your pets' home. Rats and mice love to climb and will enjoy a climbing rope, platforms and ladders. Some rats and mice also enjoy an exercise wheel. Always buy a solid wheel. Your pets' feet could be trapped and injured in a spoked wire wheel.

PET SUBJECT

Q **Can rats be house trained?**

A They can. Put a small container with some litter in the corner of the cage where the rats usually leave their droppings and wee. Add some droppings and wet litter from the cage. Make sure the litter in the container is different from what's in the rest of the cage. Place the rat in the litter tray so it knows it is there and has a sniff. If you see your rat using the tray, give it lots of praise and a favourite treat. But don't be cross with your rat if it doesn't use the tray. Just keep placing it and its droppings in the tray and it will get the idea.

Bringing your pets home

When you collect your pets you will need a container so you can carry them home safely. A plastic carrier, available at pet shops, is better than a cardboard box.

It's surprising how quickly rats and mice can chew through card. A plastic carrier will be useful for visits to the vet and as a safe place to put your pets while you are cleaning their cage.

Remember that your pets have left their mother and brothers and sisters for the first time and will feel nervous and scared. If possible, take some bedding from their old home so they have a familiar smell around them. When you get them home put them in their new cage and let them settle and explore for a while.

A plastic carrier is the best way to bring your pet home safely.

PET SUBJECT

Q **Why does my rat leave little drops of wee as he runs around?**

A The rat is leaving its scent as messages to other rats. Having its own smell around it makes a rat feel more comfortable. A scent trail helps a rat find its way as it can follow scent trails. You may find that your rat marks you as well as objects in your home!

Other animals

If you already have a pet cat or dog, introduce your pet rats or mice very carefully. Your cat or dog will see the rats or mice as prey animals – that's natural – and may frighten the rodents. But in time pets can get used to each other and rats, particularly, can become friendly with other animals. Never leave them alone together, though.

Feeding your mouse

Wild mice love to eat seeds and grain, and your pet mouse will do very well on a mixture of these foods. You can buy these at the pet shop – make sure you buy types suitable for rodents.

Mice enjoy some fresh foods such as small pieces of carrot, apple and broccoli. Wash fruit and vegetables well before giving them to your pets. You can also give your mouse some dog biscuits to chew, which will keep their teeth from growing too long. Remove uneaten food and wash the food bowls daily. Your pet also needs fresh water every day. A drip-feed bottle is best as it keeps the water clean and can't be knocked over.

20

MOUSE FACT
Pet mice are between 15 and 20 cm long, including the tail, and they weigh 30-60 grams.

Mice enjoy having a variety of different foods to eat.

Speedy runners

Mice can run fast – up to 12 km/h. In the wild mice need to be able to move quickly to escape from predators such as hawks and owls. So be careful when you let your mouse out of its cage and make sure it can't escape.

Be careful not to let your mouse run outside or underneath furniture where you can't reach it.

PET SUBJECT

Q Do mice really like cheese?

A Mice will eat almost anything that comes their way and most will certainly gobble up cheese given the chance. But cheese and other dairy foods are really too rich for mice and not very good for them. A little piece of apple is a much healthier treat.

Feeding your rat

Rats will eat almost anything and you need to take care that your pets don't eat too much and get fat.

You can buy prepared mixes for rats at pet shops and these give them a good basic diet. Your rats will also like some fresh food, something to chew, such as dog biscuits, and some scraps such as bread, pieces of cooked chicken and an occasional hard-boiled egg.

RAT FACT
A pet rat can be up to 28 cm long, with a tail that's about 23 cm long. It weighs about 450 grams – the same as a pot of jam.

22

Always buy dried mixes for rats for your pet and don't give it food meant for other types of rodent. Rats enjoy treats such as a hard-boiled egg from time to time.

PET SUBJECT

Q **My rat is sneezing. Can rats catch colds?**

A Yes, they are not quite like the colds we catch, but rats can suffer from infections that affect their breathing and make them sneeze. If your rat seems unwell and is having trouble breathing make sure you take it to the vet as soon as possible for treatment.

Learning a name

You can teach your pet rat to recognize its name. Make a little clicking sound to get your pet's attention, then repeat its name over and over. When your pet comes to your hand at the sound of its name, reward it with a little food treat. Soon your pet will realize that you are talking to it when you say its name.

Don't feed your rat treats with lots of salt or sugar. They can make it ill.

Exercise and playtime

Mice and rats need plenty of activity and enjoy having ropes, ladders and platforms to climb on inside their cage. Give them tubes to run through and cardboard boxes to hide in and chew.

An untreated branch from a fruit tree is good for rats and mice to climb on and chew. Your pets will also enjoy exercise outside their cage and this is particularly important for rats, as they are larger animals.

Many rats will happily sit on your lap and shoulder. Always make sure your home is safe for your pets. Don't let them near wires they could chew. Close doors and windows and watch out for holes your pets could squeeze into.

A unit like this is lots of fun for your pets – and you can enjoy watching them play.

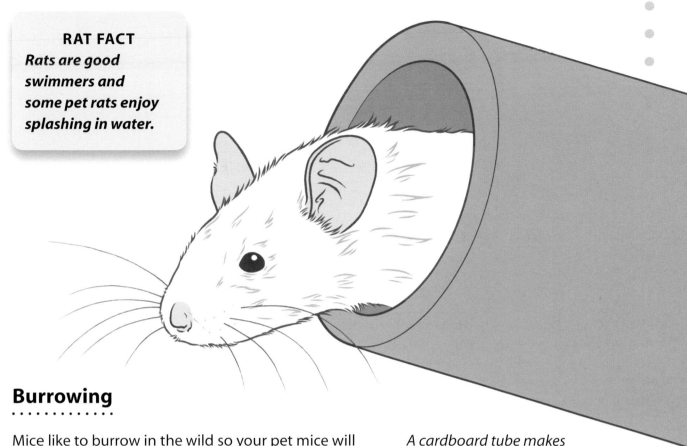

RAT FACT
Rats are good swimmers and some pet rats enjoy splashing in water.

Burrowing

Mice like to burrow in the wild so your pet mice will enjoy a chance to dig in earth, too. Fill a cardboard box with some garden soil and let your mice have fun digging and tunnelling.

A cardboard tube makes a great plaything for rats and mice.

PET SUBJECT

Q Why does my mouse eat its own poo?

A Both rats and mice sometimes eat their own poo. This is because it is hard for them to digest some of the plant food they eat. If the food passes through their system again they can extract more of the vitamins and goodness from it. This is something many rodents and rabbits do and is perfectly normal behaviour.

Handling rats and mice

Always handle your pets gently and carefully so they learn to trust you and feel comfortable. It is very frightening for any animal to be suddenly grabbed from above and held tightly.

Never pick up a mouse by the tip of its tail. Hold it firmly at the base of the tail while you slide your other hand under its body, then scoop it up with both hands. Hold it close and be very careful not to drop it.

RODENT FACT
Both rats and mice have 16 strong teeth for chewing food.

Keep your mouse safe on your hand by holding its tail firmly but gently.

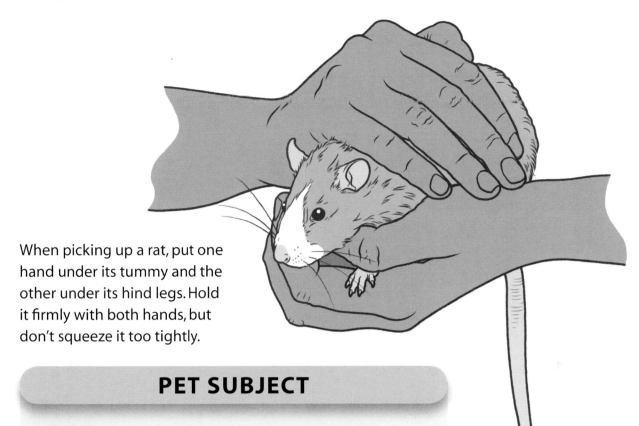

When picking up a rat, put one hand under its tummy and the other under its hind legs. Hold it firmly with both hands, but don't squeeze it too tightly.

PET SUBJECT

Q **What's the best way to make friends with my pet?**

A Try carrying a rat or mouse inside your jumper in the house when you first get your pets. That way it will get used to your smell and learn to trust you and know that you mean safety and comfort.

Hammocks

Rats love to have a range of different spots where they can sit and lie in their cage and will enjoy a cosy hammock. You can buy soft fleecy hammocks in a pet shop or make your own with an old towel or jumper. Sew some curtain hooks at each end so you can hang the hammock from the cage bars.

For parents and carers

Caring for any pet is a big responsibility. Looking after an animal takes time and money, and children cannot do everything by themselves. You'll need to show your child how to behave around animals, provide what the pets need, and make sure that they are healthy and cared for by the vet.

That said, helping to look after a pet and learning how to respect it and be gentle in handling it is very good for children and can be great fun too.

CHOOSING RATS AND MICE
Be careful to choose healthy animals. If you buy rats or mice from a pet shop you'll need to take them to the vet as soon as possible for a health check. Ask the vet to double-check the sex of the animals too. Pet shops sometimes get it wrong! Don't be tempted to keep a mixed sex group. Rats and mice start breeding very young and produce litters frequently.

If you find your pets at a rescue centre, be prepared for the centre to ask lots of questions about your life and your home. Don't be concerned about this – they are trying to do the best for their animals and to make sure that you have a pet that suits you.

Bear in mind that some children are allergic to rats and mice. Before choosing a pet, arrange for your child to handle a friend's pet or animals at a pet shop or rescue centre just in case he or she has an allergy. Fibre in the bedding can also cause breathing problems for some children.

HOUSING

You'll need to organize a cage for your pets, which can be quite expensive. You'll also need to provide bedding and help your child clean out the animals' home regularly. The animals' cage must be kept clean or your pets will suffer – and they will smell.

FEEDING

Once your pets are settled a child can bring them dry food and change their water daily. Children can give the animals their fresh food too, but make sure they know what is safe for them to eat.

HANDLING

It's very important to show children how to handle a rat or mouse properly and to learn that it is not a cuddly toy. If a child handles an animal roughly it will be nervous and insecure, so unlikely ever to be a loving pet. Teach your children to respect animals and always treat them gently. Don't let a child grab a rat or mouse and speak loudly, especially at first when the animal will be anxious. If you want your pets to be tame and friendly, you and your children will need to make sure they are handled and given attention every day. If they are left in their cage day after day they will soon become bored and nervous of humans.

HEALTH CHECK

Keep an eye on your pets' health and watch for signs of illness. Check regularly for signs of parasites such as mites or lice (you might notice scabs on the animal's skin) and claws which are growing too long. Take your pet to the vet if its claws need clipping. Look out for lumps or tumours, which are quite common in older rats and mice. They can be removed if caught early but can get very sore if they are not treated.

Glossary

breeder
Someone who keeps rats or mice and sells the young they produce.

droppings
Mice or rat poo.

grooming
Cleaning the fur.

infections
Illnesses that rats can catch from each other.

litter
A group of young from the same mother.

mammals
A group of animals that includes dogs, cats and humans, as well as rats and mice. Most mammals have four legs and some hair on the body. Female mammals feed their babies with milk from their own bodies.

parasites
Tiny creatures such as fleas, lice and mites, which can live on a mouse or rat's body.

predator
An animal that kills and eats other animals.

prey
Animals that are hunted and eaten by other animals.

rodents
A group of mammals that includes rats and mice as well as guinea pigs.

territory
An animal's home area where it spends most of its time.

vitamins
Vitamins are contained in food and help keep animals healthy.

Websites

www.rspca.org.uk/
The Royal Society for the Prevention of Cruelty to Animals (RSPCA) aims to protect animals and prevent mistreatment. The website has excellent advice about caring for your pets.

www.pdsa.org.uk/
The People's Dispensary for Sick Animals (PDSA) provides free veterinary help and advice for those in need. The website gives lots of advice on caring for pets.

http://www.bbc.co.uk/cbbc/wild/pets/
The Children's BBC website provides information aimed at children about pet care.

www.allaboutpets.org.uk/
The Blue Cross helps rehome pets and provides veterinary care. The website has useful leaflets on the care of rats, mice and other pets.

www.fancy-rats.co.uk/home/
This website has lots of information on caring for pet rats.

www.miceandrats.com/
The website of a club for owners and breeders of pet mice and rats. They also organize shows for rats and mice.

Index